ISBN : 0-7651-9184-9

Title of the French edition :
Imagerie des animaux
English translation by Translate-A-Book, a division of Transedition Limited, Oxford, England
Printed in France
Distributor in the USA : SMITHMARK Publishers Inc
115 west 18th street, New York NY 10011
Distributor in Canada : Prologue Inc
1650 Bd Lionel Bertrand, Boisbriand, Québec J7H4N7

IMAGES

All about animals

Concept:
Emilie Beaumont

Pictures:
Lindsey Selley

The hen sits on the eggs to hatch chicks.

The chick cracks the egg with its beak to get out.

hen

chick

As soon as the sun rises, the rooster crows and wakes up the farm.

The rooster, hen and chicks sleep in the hen-house.

rooster

The mother duck and her ducklings like swimming in the water.

Ducklings are very good at digging up worms.

drake

duck

ducklings

Wild geese fly away to warm countries at the end of the summer.

Flocks of geese are kept on some farms.

gander

goose

gosling

The rabbits live in a house called a hutch.

Rabbits like to eat carrots and lettuce leaves.

rabbits

young rabbits

The turkey struts about showing off his beautiful tail.

The turkey makes a gobbling noise.

turkey

turkey chick

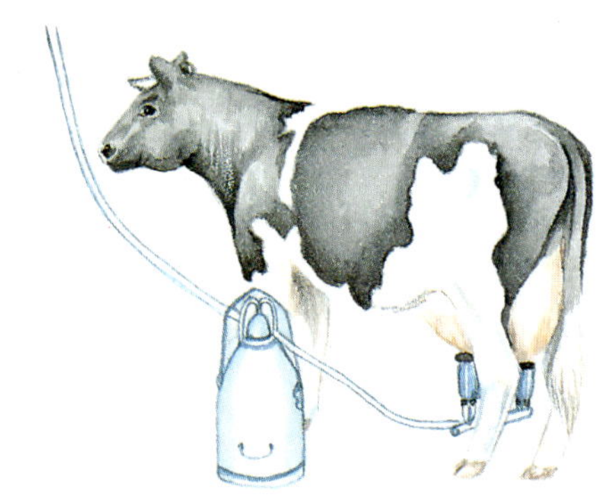

Today, cows are milked by a machine.

We make cheese, yogurt and butter from the milk.

cow

calf

The cows, calves and bulls live in cowshed.

A rodeo is a competition of cowboy skills.

bull

This horse is trained to perform at the circus.

This horse and its rider are show-jumping.

horse

foal

The donkey is very strong and can carry heavy loads.

Donkeys can be very stubborn. It's sometimes hard to make them move.

donkey

foal

A mother pig is called a sow.

Pigs love digging in the mud.

pig

piglet

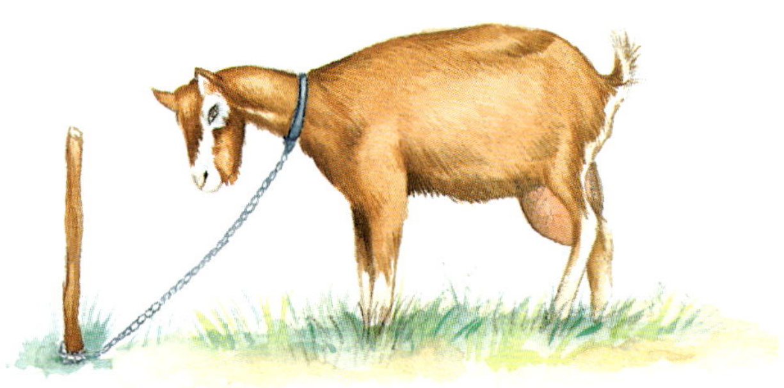

The nanny-goat bleats.

Goats' milk makes good cheese.

nanny-goat

billy-goat

kid

A group of sheep is called a flock.

Every year, sheep are shorn for their wool.

ewe

ram

lamb

The wild boar hunts for his food at night.

The wild boar has very big teeth which he uses to protect himself.

wild boar

young wild boar

FARM ANIMALS
Can you name the
animals in this picture?

During the winter, the wolf's fur becomes a much lighter color.

Wolves usually hunt at night. Their howls frighten small animals.

wolf

wolf-cub

The fox lives in a home called a den.

Foxes often try to steal chickens from farms.

fox

fox-cubs

A young deer is called a fawn.
It has a white speckled coat.

The fawn's antlers begin to grow when it is one year old.

doe

fawn

Every winter the stag's antlers fall out, but they soon grow again.

Stags often fight to protect their territory.

stag

The squirrel builds a nest with sticks and leaves.

Squirrels love to eat all sorts of nuts.

squirrel

The weasel often steals and eats birds' eggs.

Weasels hunt moles, rats and mice.

weasel

The skunk is a small and very smelly animal.

Skunks can cause a lot of damage in the hen-house.

skunk

The badger sleeps underground during the day and hunts at night.

Badgers sometimes catch frogs on the river bank.

badger

The bear digs out honey from the bees' nest in the hollow tree.

Bears are good at fishing and like eating fish.

bear

bear-cub

The panda mostly eats bamboo shoots.

Pandas are great acrobats and are very good at climbing trees.

panda and panda-cub

FOREST ANIMALS
Can you name the animals in this picture?

Mice will eat almost any kind of food. They will also gnaw at paper, plastic and wood.

mouse

rat

The vole collects food and stores it in its burrow.

Voles make lots of underground tunnels.

vole

The shrew hunts insects to eat.

Shrews sleep in holes in walls or in old tree trunks.

shrew

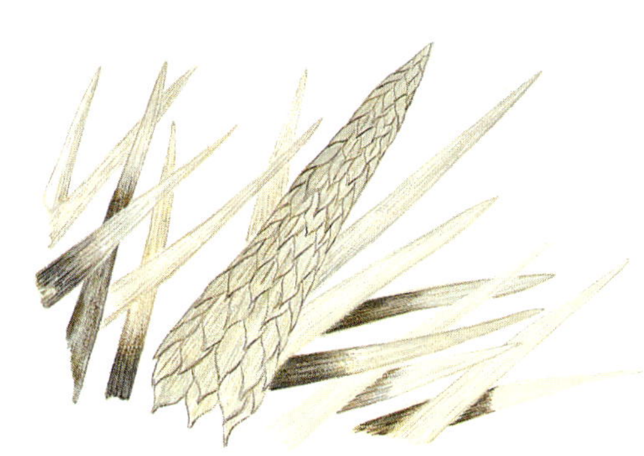

The porcupine's quills are hollow. They rattle when it shakes them.

The porcupine displays its quills and runs backwards at predators.

porcupine

A wild rabbit lives
in a warren.

Rabbits can cause a lot of
damage to cereal crops.

wild rabbit

The hare lives in a hollow.

Hares can run very fast because of their long back feet.

hare

Moles are almost blind. They dig out tunnels with their front paws.

The earth they push behind them makes mole-hills.

mole

Lizards like to lie on stones and bask in the sun.

If a lizard loses the end of its tail, it can grow back again!

lizard

earthworm

The snail's home is the shell on its back.

Snails lay little white eggs in a hole in the ground.

slug

snail

The caterpillar goes through many changes before it turns into a beautiful butterfly.

butterfly

ANIMALS OF THE COUNTRYSIDE

Name the animals in this picture.

Baby frogs are called tadpoles.

Frogs have very strong back legs and can jump a long way.

frog

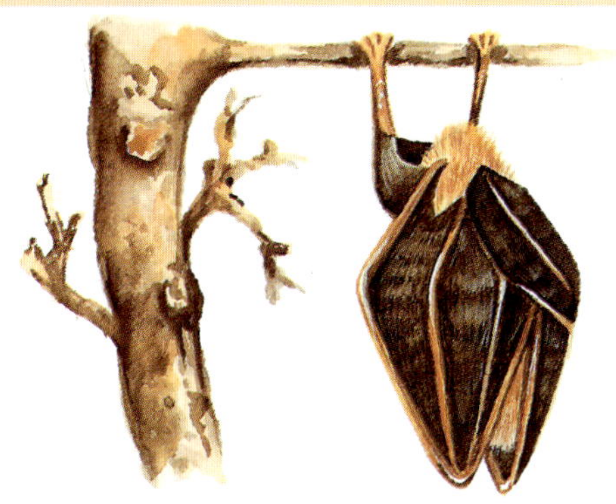

Bats sleep during the day, hanging upside down by their feet.

Bats catch insects to eat while they are flying.

bat

The beaver can make a tree fall down by gnawing its trunk.

Beavers build dams across rivers, using twigs and mud.

beaver

The raccoon washes its food before eating it.

Raccoons are very good at climbing trees.

raccoon

The otter often swims on its back when it is tired.

Otters dive deep into the water to catch fish.

otter

Some wild ducks fly south to warmer countries at the end of summer.

Wild ducks sometimes hide in the reeds.

wild duck

The heron is a type of bird called a wader. It has big feet, a long neck and a long beak. Herons live beside water.

heron

Some warblers build their nests among the reeds.

The kingfisher dives very quickly to catch fish.

warbler

kingfisher

ANIMALS OF THE WATERWAYS
Name the animals in this picture.

Wild pheasants live in fields and bushes.

On some farms, pheasants are reared with the hens and ducks.

hen pheasant

golden pheasant

Partridge chicks love to catch ants.

Partridges like to eat green grass.

partridge

These pigeons sleep in a pigeon-loft. They coo quietly.

Homing pigeons always find their way home, wherever they set off from.

pigeon

Gulls fly around fishing boats trying to steal fish from the day's catch.

seagull

Robin red-breast builds a nest in the tree branches.

Many birds feed themselves on insects.

robin

The woodpecker taps its beak on the tree trunk to find insects.

The titmouse builds its nest in the hollows of old trees.

woodpecker

titmouse

The blackbird begins to sing at dawn.

The crow loves to peck up freshly sown grain in the fields.

blackbird

crow

The magpie often steals eggs from other birds' nests.

Magpies love shiny objects and sometimes steal jewelry.

magpie

Sparrows usually live in large, noisy flocks.

Sparrows love to eat grapes.

sparrow

Swallows build their nests under the eaves of houses.

At the end of summer, swallows gather together to fly to warmer regions.

swallow

Parrots usually live for many years. Some parrots can learn to repeat words and sounds.

parrots

The budgerigar is a member of the parrot family.

Caged canaries usually eat seeds.

budgerigar

canary

The eagle builds its nest in rocks high up in the mountains.

Eagles are good hunters and catch prey in their talons.

eagle

Owls sleep during the day and hunt at night.

Tawny owls often catch little mice to eat.

tawny owl

The mother pelican stores fish in her beak to feed to her baby.

Pelicans have very strong, large wings.

pelican

A flamingo has to run along the ground before it can take off and fly.

Flamingoes eat seaweed and small shellfish.

flamingo

Storks often build their nests on top of chimneys.

Storks like to live in warm regions all the year.

stork

Swans are very beautiful birds, but they can be bad-tempered.

Swans usually build nests beside lakes or ponds.

swan

Baby crocodiles hatch from eggs and their mothers carry them to the water.

The crocodile is a good swimmer and glides noiselessly through the water.

crocodile

Baby scorpions ride on their mother's back.

Chameleons use their long tongue to catch insects.

chameleon

scorpion

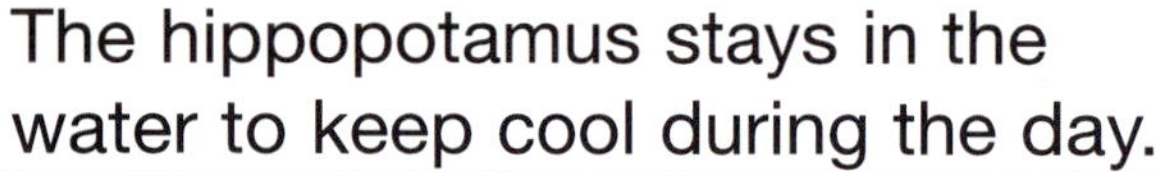

The hippopotamus stays in the water to keep cool during the day.

At night it goes searching for grass to eat.

hippopotamus

These birds are eating parasites which they find on the rhinoceros's skin.

The rhinoceros may have one or two horns.

rhinoceros

The gazelle feeds mainly on leaves from trees.

Gazelles can run very fast to escape from danger.

gazelle

The zebra's stripes help it to hide in the long grass.

Zebras eat grass, just like horses do.

zebra

A dromedary is a camel with one hump.

The dromedary can run for a whole day without stopping.

dromedary

The bactrian camel has two big humps of fat on its back.

The camel has to kneel down to allow its rider to climb on.

bactrian camel

The elephant is the biggest land animal and can live to be one hundred years old. Elephants are often hunted for their ivory tusks.

elephant

The giraffe has to spread out its front legs so it can bend down to drink the water.

These giraffes are stretching their long necks to reach leaves high up in the trees.

giraffe

The orangutan is a member of the gorilla family.

Orangutans eat fruit and leaves.

gorilla

The gorilla is the biggest and strongest of all the apes.

People sometimes train chimps to behave like humans.

Howler monkeys give out loud cries which can be heard all over the jungle.

chimpanzee

howler monkey

The sable fox lives in
the desert.

The jackal hunts for
food at night.

jackal

sable fox

The aardvark, or anteater, catches and eats ants with its long, sticky tongue.

anteater

Gnus, or wildebeests, live in a herd. They can walk for days and days to find water and grazing land.

gnu

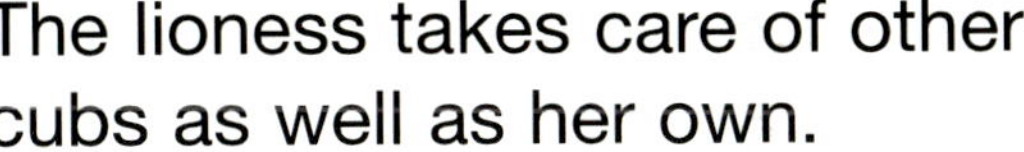

The lioness takes care of other cubs as well as her own.

Sometimes she carries her cubs in her mouth.

lion

lioness

Leopards carry the food they have caught to the tops of trees.

The black panther is the rarest kind of leopard.

leopard

The cheetah is one of the fastest animals in the world.

The tiger is a fearsome hunter. It leaps out on its prey.

cheetah

tiger

The kangaroo's baby lives in a pouch on its stomach.

Kangaroos have strong back legs with which they leap along the ground.

kangaroo

Koala bears sleep while holding onto tree trunks.

Koala bears never drink water. They eat eucalyptus leaves instead.

koala bear

ANIMALS FROM HOT COUNTRIES

Name the animals in this picture.

Boa constrictors are very strong. They squeeze their prey to death.

When snakes grow, they shed their skin because it is too small.

boa constrictor

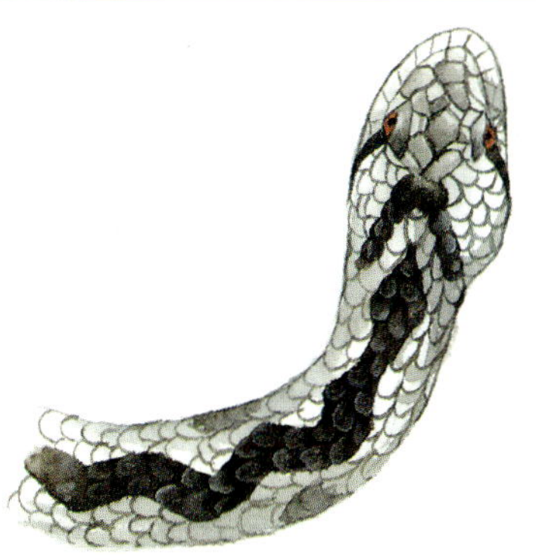

A viper can always be recognized by the ‘v’ on top of its head.

Grass snakes live in damp places and are not dangerous.

grass snake

viper

The chamois deer lives high up in the mountains.

The chamois is very agile and jumps easily from rock to rock.

chamois deer

The marmot lives in a burrow.
In winter it hibernates.

The mountain hare's coat turns completely white in winter.

marmot

mountain hare

Bees live in a hive where they make honey.

Bees gather pollen from flowers.

bee

wasp

Ants build anthills to live in.

Sometimes ants catch insects and small caterpillars which they carry to the anthill.

ant

fly

mosquito

beetle

maybeetle

cockroach

grasshopper

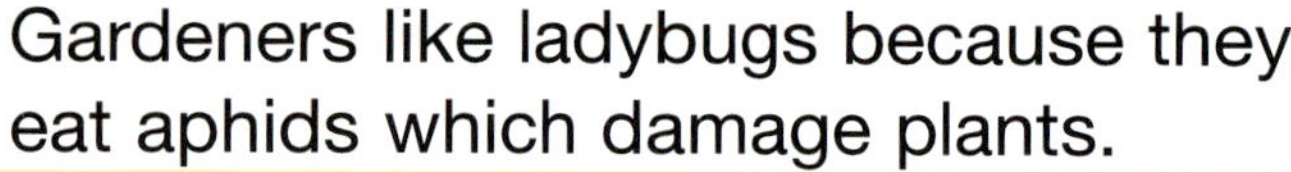

Gardeners like ladybugs because they eat aphids which damage plants.

The dragonfly is the fastest of all flying insects.

dragonfly

ladybug

Spiders spin webs to capture insects to eat.

The tarantula is an enormous spider, big enough to catch mice.

spider

RIVER FISH
perch
carp

trout
eel

sardines
skate
flounder

SEA FISH
mackerel
tuna
salmon

The whale calf feeds on its mother's milk.

Whales rise to the surface of the sea to blow out water and take in air.

whale

The shark is a fierce fish with hundreds of very sharp teeth.

Sometimes people tame dolphins and train them to do tricks.

dolphin

shark

crab

hermit crab

spider crab

octopus

lobster

crayfish

We can make jewelry with the pearls found inside some oysters.

Scallops move along the sea bed by opening and closing their shells.

oysters

cockles

mussels

Starfish have five arms. If one breaks off, they can grow another.

Beware of jellyfish because some are poisonous.

jellyfish

shrimp

starfish

whelks

ANIMALS ON ICE
walrus
penguins

polar bear
seal
sea-lion

The polar bear hunts seals on the ice.

Despite its size, the polar bear is a very fast swimmer.

polar bear

The reindeer uses its antlers to scratch in the earth for food.

Reindeer are often used to pull sleighs.

reindeer

Most small cats are domestic and spend their lives with humans, but there are some wild cats who live in the woods.

cat

Siamese cat

Persian cat

Abyssinian cat

tabby cat

Sheep-dogs are trained to take care of sheep.

Sometimes dogs sleep in their own houses called kennels.

German shepherd dog

puppy

boxer dog

fox terrier

cocker spaniel

mongrel

turtle

goldfish

guinea pig

hamster

EXTINCT ANIMALS

mammoth

Dinosaurs
stegosaurus

dimorphodon
diplodocus

tyrannosaurus

INDEX

Produced in the E.U.
by ***Partenaires-Livres®***
on SCA paper